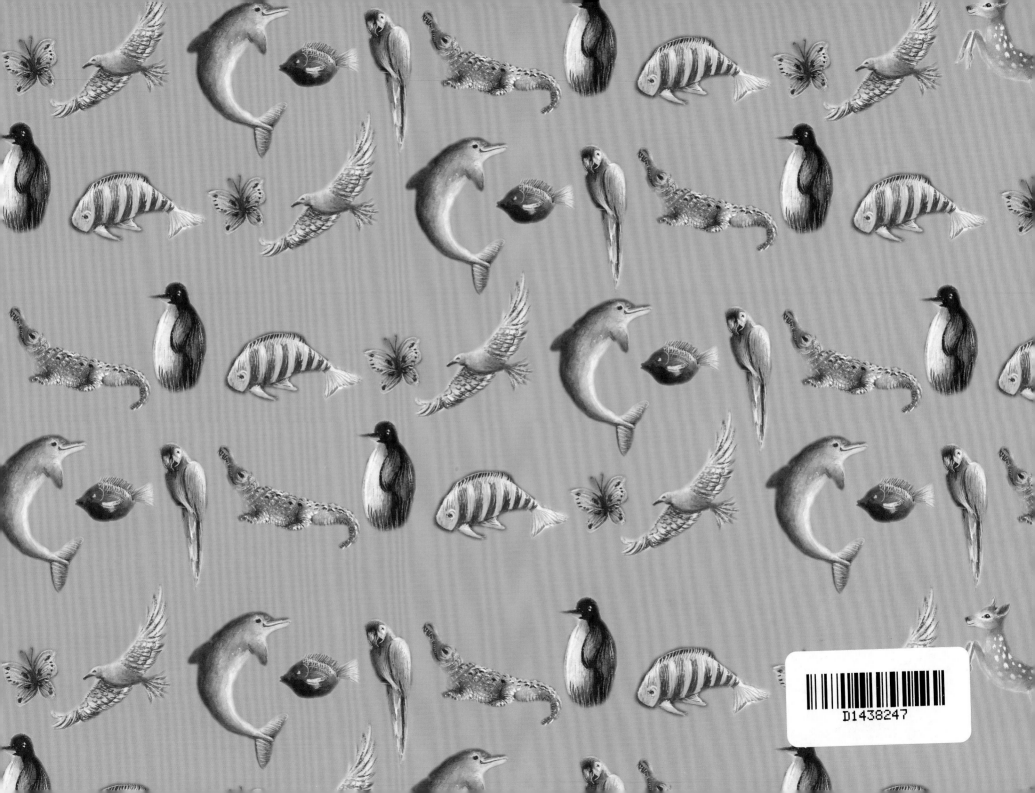

The Islamic Foundation. 2009 / 1430H

MUSLIM CHILDREN'S LIBRARY
A Trust of Treasures

Author Mehded Maryam Sinclair
Editor Farah Alvi
Illustrator Angela Desira
Cover/Book design & Layout Nasir Cadir
Coordinator Anwar Cara

Published by
THE ISLAMIC FOUNDATION
Markfield Conference Centre, Ratby Lane, Markfield
Leicestershire, LE67 9SY, United Kingdom
T: +44 (0)1530 249 230 F: +44 (0)1530 249 656
E: publications@islamic-foundation.com W: www.kubepublishing.com

Quran House, PO Box 30611, Nairobi, Kenya

PMB 3193, Kano, Nigeria

Distributed by
Kube Publishing Ltd.

A catalogue record of this book is available from the British Library.

Revised Paperback
ISBN-13: 978-0-86037-712-2
First impression, 2019.

A Trust of Treasures

MEHDED MARYAM SINCLAIR

Illustrated by **ANGELA DESIRA**

But there was no one to stand still and listen, and say "Ahhh."
The stars were whirling and glittering in the night sky,
But there was no one to be dazzled by them and discern their patterns.
The moon was waxing and waning in its orbit,
But there was no one to measure its phases or count their days by it.

The salty ocean waves were crashing on the shore,
But there was no one to sail upon them, no one to
dive in the deep waters beneath them.

The gold was veiled in the stream beds and the rocks,
But there was no one to mine it and make it into bracelets and rings.
The iron ore was sleeping in stone,
But there was no one to extract it, or smelt it into steel

The rivers of the world were full of fish,
But there was no one to roast them and grow strong from them.

The fields were rolling with shimmering wheat,
But there was no one to harvest, grind, and bake it into bread.

08

The grasslands were dappled with wild rose,
But there was no one to smell it, and no one to gather the rosehips for tea.

The camels were lurching through the desert,
But there was no one to drive them, or load them, or tease them onward.

The fat deer were skipping and cavorting in the forests,
But there was no one to catch sight of their flashing white tails.

The cliffs of gleaming white stone arched towards the sky,
But there was no one to pry away their slabs and chisel them into blocks for building.

The thorn-bushes were snatching the soft fleece from the sheep,
But there was no one to gather it, spin it, and weave it into fabric.

The bees were buzzing in their honeycombs,
But there was no one to find their honey and drizzle it on their bread.

The ants were tunneling their perfect tunnels through the sand,
But there was no one to marvel at their order.

The Power of the One was creating all of this,
But there was no one to understand why, and no one to give thanks, and no one to praise.
Then the One brought Adam, with intellect and heart,
And taught him the names of all things and gave him understanding.

16

He showed him how to look after the earth and all its wonderful creatures, to make use of its bounties, to take only what is needed and not be wasteful, and to replenish what he used.

And so Adam fulfilled his duty as God's representative on earth, bowing down to His Majesty and giving thanks to Him.

And Adam's children, and his children's children,
and his children's children's children down through the ages, all the way to us,
Have been called upon to reflect and rise up to his example, to respect and care
for our earth and give praise and thanks to its Creator.

The bees are still buzzing in their honeycombs,
And we gather their honey and drizzle it on our bread.
The thorn-bushes are still snatching the soft fleece from the sheep,
And we gather it, spin it, and weave it into fabric.

The cliffs of gleaming white stone are still arching towards the sky,
And we pry away their slabs and chisel them into blocks for building.

The camels are still lurching through the desert,
And we drive them, and load them, and tease them onward.

The grasslands are still dappled with wild rose,
And we smell it, and gather the rosehips for tea.
The fields are still rolling with shimmering wheat,
And we harvest, grind, and bake it into bread.

22

The rivers of the world are still full of fish,
And we catch them, roast them, and grow strong from them.

23

The iron ore is still sleeping in stone,
And we extract it and smelt it into steel.
The gold is still veiled in the stream beds and the rocks,
And we mine it and make it into bracelets and rings.

The salty ocean waves are still crashing on the shore,
And we sail upon them in fine ships, and dive the deep waters beneath them.

The moon is still waxing and waning in its orbit,
And we measure its phases and count our days by it.
The stars are still whirling and glittering in the night sky,
And we are dazzled by them and love their patterns.
The universe is still humming praise for its Creator,
And we stand still to hear, and are astonished.

The Power of the One is still creating all of this, even as we live and breathe.
And like Adam, peace upon him, we bow down in love and awe.
We hold the trust that the mountains and even the angels feared to take.
Our work is to remember, and remembering, to cherish and protect and give thanks.